Prayers of Hope, Words of Courage

GW00471983

PRAYERS
of HOPE
WORDS *of* COURAGE

By
Francis Xavier
Nguyễn Văn Thuận

Pauline
BOOKS & MEDIA
Boston

Library of Congress Cataloging-in-Publication Data

Nguyễn, Francis Xavier Văn Thuận, 1928-
  Prayers of hope, words of courage / by Francis Xavier Nguyễn Văn Thuận.
    p. cm.
  ISBN 0-8198-5938-9 (pbk.)
  1. Meditations. 2. Catholic Church—Prayer-books and devotions—English. I. Title.
  BX2182.3 .N47 2002
  242'.802—dc21

                                2002002638

Cover image: adapted from a photograph by Sr. M. Emmanuel Alves, FSP

Printed and published in the U.S.A. by Pauline Books & Media, 50 Saint Pauls Avenue, Boston, MA 02130-3491.

www.pauline.org

Pauline Books & Media is the publishing house of the Daughters of St. Paul, an international congregation of women religious serving the Church with the communications media.

2 3 4 5 6 7 8 9   09 08 07 06 05 04 03

Contents

Preface

In the silence of my prison cell I thought of all of the faithful friends who were praying for me: simple people, especially children, from several countries, people who had never seen me and yet wrote to me to testify to their affection. Each year at Christmas I received hundreds of postcards, often homemade, from so many people expressing thoughts, which touched me deeply. I wondered how I could show my gratitude to all of these people. I had nothing in prison, not so much as a stamp, and above all no freedom. Despite my extreme poverty, I still had one thing: the love of Christ in my heart; I was very rich indeed. And so, I wrote this book as a testimony of my love and gratitude to them. How was I able to write in prison? Love can do all things.

During my imprisonment, I wanted to love my young prison guards sincerely. Initially, they did not believe me. But after many years together, we became friends in Christ. When I conceived of the idea of writing this book, I asked, "May I write my meditations and prayers and take them with me when I leave this prison?"

"That is forbidden! You cannot take so much as a pair of chopsticks out of here!"

"But you know that my writings are not political."

"We understand, but we are not the ones who will examine your belongings when you leave. Your writings will certainly be confiscated!"

I appealed to their hearts: "The reason I dare to ask you so sincerely is because I have confidence in you."

"Well then, write in a foreign language under the pretext of doing exercises in order not to forget it by the time you get out of prison."

And that is just what I did. I wrote on scraps of paper that my guards provided. I made a cover from a page of a newspaper and wrote on it: *Foreign Language Study*. I chose to write my thoughts in Italian because in Vietnam it is a language less commonly known than English or French.

I have left the text as I wrote it in prison, from day to day, without regrouping the subjects. The volume contains ninety meditations and prayers.* I am aware that there are many mistakes in it, but it is a remembrance of the year 1987, and the expression of my profound gratitude.

The Scriptures used are not from any specific translation, since the author did not have a copy of the Bible with him in prison and had to quote from memory. Citations are provided for the reader at the end of each meditation or prayer.

Mary, my Mother

Mary, Mother of Jesus, my Mother,
  I want to call you *our* Mother
  to feel close to Jesus
  and to all my brothers and sisters,
  Come live in me, Mary,
    with Jesus your beloved Son,
  in silence and in waiting,
  in prayer and in offering,
  in communion with the Holy Trinity
    and the Church,
  in the fervor of your *Magnificat,*
  that message of complete renewal;
  in union with Joseph, your most holy spouse;
  in your humble and loving work
    to accomplish Jesus' will;
  in your love for Jesus, for Joseph,
  for the Church, and for all humanity;
  in your unshakeable faith
  in the midst of so many trials
    endured for the kingdom;
  in your ceaselessly active hope,
  to build a new world of righteousness and peace,
  of happiness and true tenderness;
  in the perfection of your virtues
    in the Holy Spirit,

so as to become a witness of the Good News,
an apostle of the Gospel.

Continue, O Mother, to work,
to pray, to love, and to sacrifice in me;
continue to carry out the Father's will,
continue to be the Mother of humanity;
continue to live Jesus' passion
and resurrection in me.

O Mother, I consecrate myself entirely to you,
now and forever.

In living your spirit and that of Joseph,
I shall live the spirit of Jesus.

I love you, O our Mother,
with Jesus, Joseph, the angels, the saints,
and all people.

I will share your labors, your cares,
and your struggle
for the kingdom of the Lord Jesus. Amen.

*Mary, my
Mother*

An illusion

A whole stream of public opinion tells the Church to moderate its requirement of sacrifice and renunciation, to lower its expectations of priests, religious, and lay people. Some people believe that a more lenient attitude, a less demanding way of life, would attract more vocations and believers to the Church. But experience has shown that this is an illusion.

Young people want to give themselves completely, and to become authentic disciples of Christ. They want an unequivocally evangelical life and detest partial commitments and "accommodating virtue." They are not afraid of self-denial; their only fear is to undervalue the evangelical call, to live a mediocre Christian life or a stunted priestly or religious life.

Lord,
we, the youth of the whole world
turn our eyes toward you, our ideal.
Draw us to yourself.
We offer boundless thanks to you
for what you demand of us.
Thank you for giving us the freedom to choose
and for respecting our human dignity
despite our weakness.

You have saved me, Lord,
and you made me a child of God.
You are not like materialism

to which people may become slave
in their hunger for consumption,
and by following the path of false pleasures.
I will follow you alone, Lord.
I accept being a child of God
and embrace all the demands that name entails.

I am convinced. I must follow the narrow way—
the only way that leads to everlasting life.

An
illusion

❧ 3 ❧

Love your neighbor

Kneeling before your tabernacle, Lord, I hear you repeating to me, *"Love your neighbor as yourself!"* I understand what you demand of me, Lord. When I go back over my life, I see clearly how I have not yet loved anyone as I love myself. I have not yet *really* put your word into practice; I have loved others, but less than myself.

Nevertheless, I sometimes flattered myself that I was living charitably and that I was one of your authentic disciples!

St. Paul understood and lived your demand of love: *"Who is weak and I am not weak? Who is offended and I do not burn with indignation?"* He also wrote to the Church at Rome: *"Rejoice with those who rejoice, weep with those who weep."*

It is not enough to give a few coins or to help the victims of natural disasters with used clothing. I must treat my brothers and sisters as my right hand treats my left hand when it is hurt.

Cf. Mk 12:31; 2 Cor 11:29; Rom 12:15

҂ 4 ҂

God knows us

Often we try to hide our true selves from others. We hide our joys and sorrows, successes and failures, because we are afraid that others might try to aggravate our wounds. It is rare to find someone who understands us perfectly.

"No one understands me!" is a common complaint.

"O Lord, you have searched me and known me.
  You know my sitting down and my rising up.
  Where can I go from your Spirit?
  If I ascend into heaven, you are there;
  if I make my bed in hell, behold, you are there.
  If I take the wings of the morning,
  and dwell in the uttermost parts of the sea,
  you are there..."

Does the Psalmist mean here that God will pursue me, that God spies on me? No, rather: *God's hand leads me, and God's right hand holds me fast.*

Lord, you know me entirely—you know my sins and my misery not to condemn me, but to have mercy on me and to save me.

Help me to understand other people, Lord, without disdaining or criticizing them, without giving up hope for them, so that together we may sing of your love and love one another as you love us.

Cf. Ps 139

Communion and clarity

When I am so convinced about some negative aspect of my life, I sometimes sink into despair. I must put my trust in your love and abandon myself to you.

When I am so convinced about some negative aspect of another's life, I am sometimes inclined to detest them and to stay away from them.

Then I must stop to contemplate your love for me. Why do you love me, Lord, when I feel disdain and disgust for my brothers and sisters?

Give me the courage to see things as you see them, Lord, and to love unconditionally. Only then will true communion be realized.

Often, behind a facade of courtesy and attentiveness there exists a hidden dissension, which weakens communion and renders it insincere.

Lord, you are infinite patience.
  You are limitless understanding.
  Your love is eternal.

Quoniam in aeternum misericordia eius.

Do unto others

I have often thought that if I did *unto others what I would like others to do to me,* then I would have reached the perfection of charity. Then, satisfied that I had accomplished all that was necessary, I could rest from my efforts. But that is not your unit of measure, Lord.

To visit someone, to distribute help, and to bring consolation are not merely good acts to be tallied up. It is not enough to do for others—I must courageously experience their sufferings, their wounds, their deepest aspirations, humiliations, misery, and despair in my own heart. This is the Gospel.

Your teaching is so simple, Lord, and yet so profound! I must love others *"as myself"*! What depth! How can I avoid living the fullness of your law of love?

Only when I am one with my brother or sister, when I carry in my own flesh and heart the destiny of someone who is suffering in body and soul, will I truly love that person as myself. If someone strikes my brother or sister, my own flesh is bruised and wounded.

Can anyone really love like this? You answered this question a long time ago when you said: *"There is no greater love than to give one's life..."* for one's friends.

Lord, help me to remember the example of St. Maximillian Kolbe who offered to die in the place of a fellow prisoner!

Cf. Lk 6:31; Jn 15:13

꧁ 7 ꧂

A grain of sand

What do my actions mean to anyone and what are they worth? They are little drops of water in a vast ocean, tiny grains of sand in an enormous desert! But an immense ocean is composed of countless drops of water, and a boundless desert of infinite grains of sand.

Am I not dust, which is destined to return to dust? Am I not less than dust because *"I was taken from the ash heap"*?

"He raises the poor out of the dust,
  and lifts the needy out of the ash heap,
  that he may seat him with princes
  with the princes of his people."

Lord, you made me your child not only for my personal happiness, not for my own advancement, but to entrust me with a particular mission within your plan of salvation.

Lord, help me to meditate unceasingly on the advice of St. Leo the Great: *"Christian, be aware of your dignity!"*

Perhaps I am only a grain of sand, but every grain has its own place, its special role to carry out—the sole condition is my awareness of this reality and my unity with all others.

Cf. Ps 113

ℒ 8 ℒ

Three fish and two loaves

It is true that to give a few dollars to a neighbor is not such a great thing, but even a few dollars can buy a loaf of bread or a bowl of rice to satisfy the tormenting hunger of a child or elderly person. Is it not infinitely better to give that little than to allow it to disintegrate in a safe—that inexcusable crime so often committed by the very people who believe themselves virtuous?

I must see, with the eyes of Jesus, the value of what appears inadequate to me—three fish, two loaves of bread, the widow's mite...

I thought to myself, "A dollar is worthless" and I thought no further of what I could do, saying, "What good is it to rack my brain for an answer?" And thus, I was guilty of doing nothing, guilty "by omission." I sinned because I lacked a spirit of enterprise—a person with a dollar does nothing, but a million people with a dollar each! I sinned because I lacked confidence in the good will of others, in a spirit of unity. But above all, I lacked heart!

If I were truly compassionate, no obstacle, no difficulty would cause me turn back. For the sake of others, I would seek to do good not only dollar by dollar, but also penny by penny. The Congregation for the Evangelization of Peoples was born out of the efforts of Pauline Jarricot who began by collecting contributions for the work coin by coin.

ℒ 9 ℒ

Abandon security

No one—the Church or its members—can be satisfied with possessing the faith and withdrawing behind a
fortress to enjoy it with security. Rather, we cannot stop
moving forward in our search for God; and on the way,
Jesus advances and draws closer to us.

In the press of the crowds, Jesus sought out Levi, the
Samaritan woman, and the apostles who labored in their
fishing boats. Jesus seeks me in the midst of humanity—
with the rickshaw, the street sweeper, and the vendor.

From the very beginning, Christianity was called *the
way;* Jesus called himself *the Way.* I must leave the safety
of my fortress, Lord, because those who wish to follow
you are not found there. You did not ask me to shut myself behind some fortification, but to follow you.

> *Go preach the Gospel.*
> *Go into the whole world.*
> *Be my witnesses even to the ends of the earth.*
>
> Cf. Acts 9:2; Jn 4:6

❧ 10 ❧

Give unceasing thanks

There are so many gifts that are freely received: the morning dew on the grass, the light of the sun, the heat of the day, sparkling water from a fountain, the freshness of the wind, the warbling of a bird, the warmth of a friendly hand, the familiar sound of a church bell ringing.... Have I ever thought of giving thanks for all of this? I enjoy all these gifts without having paid a penny.

If I keep my eyes open and my spirit alert, I will live in continual thanksgiving. I am overwhelmed by the memory of so many graces: my mother's womb, the milk with which she nourished me, my father's labor and sweat, the knowledge and formation received from teachers, the devotion of priests whose hands blessed, pardoned, gave the Body of Christ, and imparted the anointing of the sick to my body.

Thank you, Lord, for having chosen me
    to be your child.
  Thank you for having given me Mary
    for my Mother.
  Thank you for the mission I received
    from you in the Church.
  Thank you for having revealed your mysteries
    to me.
  Thank you for so many brothers and sisters
    who sustain me.

Thank you for the people who place obstacles
    on my path and cause me trouble;
they help me to become holy.
Thank you for my birth as a Vietnamese.
Thank you for allowing me to live in
    this particular time in history.
Thank you for giving me a share
    in your bitter chalice.

I should sing your praise my whole life long for just one of these gifts. How much more praise I should give you for the innumerable graces, which I alone know, and for all the graces I am not aware of or do not remember. I will need an eternity to thank you unceasingly.

How can I repay you, Lord, for filling my life with so many good things?

Give unceasing
thanks

The Church: servant of Christ's message

The Gospel is a grace generously offered to all people. Even outside it, one can benefit from the Church.

What is essential is not the Church's prestige or profit. The essential is to free the dynamic truth of the kingdom so that it reaches all people.

The Lord Jesus advised his apostles not to oppose those who cast out demons in his name, though they did not belong to their company. Jesus wanted us to work in collaboration with everyone and not to behave like arrogant, exclusive owners of truth. Where there are love and cooperation, Jesus is found.

In the service of the Church, I will be a faithful and humble servant of Jesus' message. I will not be an exacting administrator who increases the number of obstacles and difficulties encountered along the path by people who are seeking God and, because of these obstacles, falter, despair, and turn away.

I want to be in the habit of questioning myself: Which of my words, gestures, or behaviors distances others from you, Lord? Have I disappointed or led them to mistaken ideas about the Church? Does the great number of messengers of the Gospel fill me with joy? Am I happy to work with and sustain them?

If the Church encounters difficulty moving forward in the spread of the Gospel, perhaps it is because there are too many "owners" of the Gospel, and too few faithful servants.

Cf. Lk 9:49–50

Who is the greatest?

Children, the abandoned, the isolated, and the poor must take precedence in the Church. They were the objects of Jesus' special attention—as the entire Gospel testifies. They are the objects of the Church's particular solicitude.

Those who help the most humble, who carry in their hearts the torments of others, and who give themselves in service, are Jesus' disciples.

The Church does not attach so much importance to the valuable work of this or that member, as to the urgency of the physical or spiritual misery of so many people who need help.

As long as I maintain a divisive mentality, a criterion of valuation, and habits characteristic of a bureaucratic spirit, I am not yet living the Gospel. As long as I put myself on top, and parade my good works, fasts, and almsgiving, I ridicule the unfortunate and do not truly love.

I must wake up as soon as possible and correct myself with urgency so that the path I am following will not make me a companion of *"the enemies of the cross of Christ."*

Cf. Phil 3:18

❧ 13 ❧

For me, to live is Mary and Joseph

I cannot separate Mary and Joseph from Jesus. That would be opposed to Jesus' example, who, after the Father, loved Joseph and Mary the most. And in heaven, he loves them eternally.

No one ever reflected Jesus' life more perfectly than Mary and Joseph.

If Jesus could say to Philip, *"He who sees me sees the Father,"* then I can say, "The one who sees Mary and Joseph sees Jesus." Mary and Joseph form the most faithful image of Jesus; and for this reason I can formulate the shortest path to holiness: *"For me, to live is Christ, it is Mary and Joseph."*

Mary, my mother,
  Joseph my father,
  give me your eyes to contemplate Jesus;
  give me your hearts and spirits to understand
    him,
  and to be impassioned for him.
  Give me your will so that I may work for him
  with my whole heart and mind without growing
    weary.
  Give me your soul that I may endlessly proclaim:
  "Jesus, my Lord and my all!"

Mihi vivere Iesus est, mihi vivere Maria et Ioseph.
Cf. Jn 14:9

Authentic Christianity

A Christian worthy of the name is one who imitates Jesus' life in every circumstance of his or her own life.

The life of every saint brings to light some particular mystery of Jesus' life: his childhood, his preaching, his love for children, his passion, etc. The Virgin Mary lived all the mysteries in their perfection.

The first Christians had an original way of expressing their identity:

The Christian is one who bears Jesus
   in his or her mind,
   in his or her heart,
   in his or her gaze,
   in his or her hands,
   on his or her lips,
   in his or her entire being.

A motto for life

Sometimes I want to adopt a practical way of living the Gospel, which can be condensed in a formula, one that is easy to understand, retain, and apply and would summon up all my energy. St. Paul coined such a formula for me when he said:

"For me, to live is Christ."

We read in his letters how deeply this phrase permeated St. Paul's soul.

"For if we live, we live to the Lord; and if we die, we die to the Lord. Therefore, whether we live or die, we are the Lord's. For to this end Christ died, and rose, and lived again, that he might be Lord of both the dead and the living."

"He died for all, that those who live should live no longer for themselves, but for him who died for them and rose again."

The Father declared:

"This is my beloved Son
in whom I am well pleased;
listen to him."

May Jesus continue his life in mine!

Cf. Phil 1:21; Rom 14:8, 9; 2 Cor 5:15; Lk 3:22

ℒ 16 ℒ

What is a Christian?

A Christian is a disciple of the Lord who keeps his commandments, and if not...Jesus has said openly: *"He cannot be my disciple."*

A Christian seeks God's will, the happiness of others, and new forms of the Church's presence in today's world. A Christian loves the cross of Christ and carries it in his or her life. A Christian is a living *Credo,* continuing Jesus' work here on earth, and making the song of hope resound in the midst of the world's trials.

Whatever difficulties may arise, the Christian remains God's heir.

For love of Christ, a Christian accepts hatred if it comes, and resists sin, laziness, mediocrity, and injustice.

The Holy Spirit dwells in and enlightens a Christian.

A Christian who is continually renewed makes Jesus' revolution of love alive in his or her life. With the Church, a Christian lives the passion of Christ in union with Mary, in the midst of critics, opposition, and that suffering which is destructive.

In a word, a Christian is a faithful reproduction of the life of Christ who causes all who see him or her to say, "There is Christ!"

Cf. Lk 14:26

Little things

Sometimes campaigns are organized for children and they are invited to participate in "mini-projects" to gather pieces of metal, paper, or fragments of glass to be recycled into useful materials.

Although I am older, there are many "mini-projects" which attract me, though their objective is far more vast:

Bits of time,
 household tasks,
 a friendly smile for everyone,
 a helping hand offered to a colleague,
 support given to an elderly person
  getting on a bus,
 saving water and electricity,
 efforts to avoid creating noise
 to respect others' need for silence...

When all of these small "projects" are purified in the furnace of love, there springs up around me a society filled with the joy of living.

18

Egotists

With egotists there are no meetings, only conflicts. Egotists desire to hoard and gather for themselves, indeed, they adore their *ego* and always seek more honors, pleasures, wealth, and influence. And to achieve this end, they will walk over others, push them aside, or ignore them completely.

Familiar with quarreling myself, I will not hasten to blame others; I will examine myself first to see whether I am actually the egotist.

Two pieces of iron, stone, or wood do not produce sparks on impact, but when two bombs collide, the explosion is deafening and the destruction immense.

ℒ 19 ℒ

Ordinary tasks

A rich person may not think of gathering up leftover bread and fish from his or her dinner table, but a poor person knows the value of a grain of rice. For a poor person a grain of rice is like gold, and what is gathered is not for that person alone, but to have something on hand to share with others.

I must know how to gather the most ordinary tasks to myself and to accomplish them as well as possible and with all of my love. For spiritual poverty is also careful not to lose the smallest crumb. Jesus was poor and he said, *"Gather up what remains."*

Cf. Jn 6:12

What do you seek?

Pier Giorgio Frassati was a handsome young man born into a rich family; he had everything. So much in his life could have prevented him from a radical following of Christ: the attractions of an upper class milieu, popularity, and pressure from his family. Yet, in the burning enthusiasm of his youth, he flung himself generously into his quest for Christ. He would not accept a conventional life, not even a virtuous one. He did not desire to live a spirit of service at a reduced price. He feared an apostolic life that would not divest him of a mediocre spirit, which he believed contrary to the way of the cross to which the Lord was calling him.

He wanted a commitment without conditions, worthy of an authentic disciple of Christ and a person passionate for the apostolate. He lived an exceptional life as a student, pursuing his ideals of purity, charity, and service.

And what a remarkable sight there was at his death! Spontaneously, a huge crowd knelt in silence as Pier Giorgio's coffin passed through the city on the way to the cemetery! Why was there such a display of emotion? The people knew that during his brief life, he had tried to live the Christian ideal and to follow Christ faithfully.

Now Pier Giorgio serves as a model for young people throughout the world.

Thank you, Pier Giorgio Frassati! Thank you, my young friend! You drew me in your wake when I was still a young student at my school desk.

℘ 21 ℘

The power of witness

A sign attracts attention; the more luminous, the more it stands out and the greater its impact. Such is a lighthouse shining in the darkness of night in the midst of the ocean, a red lamp at the top of a high tower or antennae, traffic lights on our city streets, flashing lights on an air field...

A sign's power lies in its "difference": a distinct color, the brilliance of a light beam, a particular sound, etc. Without this, these signals would not attract attention.

If I am not different in some way or am afraid to be, I will not be a recognizable sign. No one will pay attention to me. I will not be able to transmit any message to those who are always in a hurry and focused on so many other things.

A sign is a witness. The Lord asks me to be a sign showing the Father in heaven to all people. Perhaps it may happen that to be a witness I must scream like an ambulance siren.... But most of the time, a sign is silent. Often it is sufficient to be present—constantly, obstinately, courageously present—and never leave one's post.

ℒ 22 ℒ

The world needs witnesses

The more major a road, the more abundant and clear must be its traffic signals. If one were to take away all the traffic signs from our city streets or highways, terrible accidents would follow very quickly.

Though they are silent, signals speak clearly:
— they take the place of a human presence;
— they exercise considerable influence on social and economic life;
— they can change the direction and daily itinerary of millions of people.

Every epoch has its signs, which transform a society's way of living and thinking.

Each time you call me to, Lord, I must have the courage to be your sign, even if others show ill will or hostility toward me. There is nothing astonishing in encountering negative reactions. After all, a signal may oblige us to stop midstream, yield to another, or, indeed, commit ourselves to a new path. Perhaps one must change directions completely and abandon a road of unrighteousness or deceit that one has been following.

John the Baptist was a sign for Herod. John insisted that Herod cease living in a way contrary to God's law, to change his direction. And John the Baptist paid for this with his life.

✍ 23 ✍

An authentic witness

In every epoch, the Lord establishes signs to guide humanity. These signs are the lives of the saints. The saints are signs of purity, poverty, fidelity, courage, faith, and love. As a sign, each of their lives is a word of God as Jesus is the Word of the Father.

They may be severe guides,
    audacious and unwavering,
    like Moses and Elijah;
    pastors both venerable and wise,
    like Saints John and Athanasius,
    Cyril and Augustine;
    young yet heroic souls,
    like Saints Cecilia, Agnes, and Lucy...

Each had his or her own way of being a saint—
    a sign for their particular age—
    but all of them proclaimed to humanity:
    "There is a God. God is love.
    The Gospel is the way to the kingdom.
    Repent! Change your life!"

❦ 24 ❧

The courage to be a witness

The person who desires to become a sign must be dedicated to sacrifice, even as the aged Simeon prophesied of Jesus: *"This child...will be a sign of contradiction."*

The person who wants to be a sign will share in the destiny of the Virgin Mary: *"And a sword will pierce your soul!"*

A sign must be steady and bold,
   luminous and watchful,
   indifferent to opinions,
   well rooted and unshakeable,
   capable of facing storms and long nights,
   trials and dangers.

And if the Lord chooses you to become a sign in this present time, will you accept or refuse?

Moses and Elijah wanted to escape, but God's grace came upon them and these powerful men had to submit, for the Spirit of God was working in them.

Cf. Lk 2:34–35

❧ 25 ❧

Ave!

Ave!—Hello!

This is a simple salutation, but from the moment the Archangel Gabriel used it, this greeting was sanctified inasmuch as it is associated with the sublime mystery of salvation, inasmuch as it awakened adoration, thanksgiving, and tenderness within Mary!

Ave! This should be my salutation,
   addressed to everyone with Mary's joy.
Ave! This is an announcement of grace,
      reconciliation, renewal, and resurrection.
Ave! This is a wish of divine benediction.

I was deeply impressed with the story of a holy priest who, for love of Mary, responded *Ave* every time someone knocked on his door. At the last moment of his life, at his request, everyone who had gathered around his bed began to sing the *Magnificat: "My soul magnifies the Lord."* How many times a day during his life had he said, *Ave?* How many times, in the seventy years he lived, had his lips formed that word?

From the depths of my love,
   I want to offer you a crown, Lord,
   woven of the most beautiful *Aves* of my life,
   to make reparation for the *Ave* of Judas

that served as a sign of his betrayal *(Ave, Rabbi)*,
and for the *Ave* of the Roman soldiers
spoken in mockery *(Ave, King of the Jews)*.

Cf. Lk 1:26

Ave!

ℒ 26 ℒ

Surprises

How many times I am surprised by my slowness of mind and blindness of heart. When I open the eyes of my soul, will it be too late as it was for the rich man of the Gospel?

Until now I had not suspected
    that the powerful would be disgraced
      and the humble exalted,
    that all done for the least would be done
      unto God,
    that sadness would be changed into joy
      and death into life,
    that those who sowed in tears would reap in joy,
    that true happiness belongs to the poor in spirit,
    to those who suffer and weep,
    and to those who are persecuted
      for righteousness...

"The kingdom of heaven belongs to them"; and Lazarus the beggar who was cast out by the rich man now rests in the bosom of Abraham!

How many surprises there will be in the end. What a total reversal of what we often value!

Cf. Mk 10:14

Discoveries

In the beginning human beings lived on the fruits, plants, and roots they gathered. Then they learned to hunt and to subsist on raw meats and fish, which they later roasted, cooked, or dried. Human progress moved forward steadily.

Today, thanks to processing, we have various methods for preserving foods. We have explored the ocean, that immense reserve of food and precious minerals. We have explored the Antarctic, which is also a gigantic reserve and natural museum where we can read the history of the earth's formation and climates. We have and will continue to explore the Moon, Mars, Saturn...

In the past, people observed and studied, but were not able to find.... Today, thanks to scientific progress, new means of research, and new instruments of observation, every day we are discovering new marvels, which seemed unbelievable only yesterday.

If I continually renew my outlook and adopt Divine Revelation—which is forever new—as an instrument of my "research" then I will never cease to discover the marvels, the sublime ideals, and the unequalled resources hidden in the most ordinary things.

ℒ 28 ℒ

Seeing as God sees

Many people are surprised by the weakness of their sight: they cannot see what the saints contemplated, or perceive what the saints so easily distinguished.

This is because saints look at everything with God's eyes; they measure their existence in God's light; they do not give into confusion, because they live in reality and the truth.

It is not really so surprising when certain people cannot see as saints do, especially if material possessions and self-indulgence are the goal of their existence, and if they resort to cunning, hypocrisy, and lies for their own gain. It is no surprise when these people consider sacrifice, modesty, and patience to be foolish.

How astonished they will be when they see that *"God made use of the humble and small in order to confound the powerful."* A great many people have been confounded throughout history, and often precisely those who enjoyed an ill-gotten hour of fame.

When the supposedly invincible *Titanic* ran into a gigantic iceberg on its first ocean crossing, the passengers were also astonished when, fighting death in the icy waters, they heard the orchestra of the sinking ocean liner playing the powerful and moving strains of the canticle: "I believe in you, my God, I believe in you..."

I believe in you, Lord!

Cf. 1 Cor 1:27

Value the ordinary

By your example, Lord Jesus, you have taught me to live close to reality and to value ordinary tasks: gathering leftover loaves and fish, fishing, cooking, buying oil, visiting the abandoned and sick, sharing food and clothes, loving, pardoning those who do me wrong...many completely ordinary responsibilities!

Each of us carries out ordinary tasks every day, but the range of their influence is immense. Ordinary tasks can bring life and happiness to a person, provoke a family's collapse, or even prepare a new society for the future.

Such tasks bear witness to our love and, if done for the Lord, serve as a key that opens the doors of paradise. Who proclaimed this? Jesus himself when he said: *"Whoever is faithful in the small things will also be faithful in the great."*

Ordinary things await us at every moment of life. If we all accomplished our humble tasks with the heart of Jesus, his revolution of love would be complete and success would be in our hands!

My surprise and joy will be great when I hear Jesus say to me, *"Well done, good and faithful servant; you have been faithful in the little things.... Enter into the joy of your Lord."*

Cf. Lk 16:10; Mt 25:21

The struggle in every moment

Love leads to communion,
   and communion allows everyone
   to move forward in harmony.
   Communion is not a happiness
   passively enjoyed,
   but it struggles to maintain a fraternal spirit
   and to open the doors of this fraternity
     to all people.

By nature, love propagates itself;
   it is contagious, communicates to others,
   and draws everyone toward communion.

I must engrave this maxim within myself:
   "Communion is the struggle of every moment."
   A moment's neglect can destroy it;
   a mere trifle suffices,
   a single thought without charity,
   an obstinately maintained prejudice,
   a harmful attachment,
   an erroneous direction,
   a personal ambition or interest,
   an action done for myself and not for the Lord,
   returning to a bad habit already abandoned,
   the desire for personal satisfaction
   that overrides what is pleasing to the Lord.

Help me, Lord, to examine myself in this way:
  Who is the center of my life: you or me?
  If you are the center, then everyone
    will be gathered into unity.
  But if, instead, I see that people around me
    lose interest and disperse,
  that will be a sign that I have put myself
    at the center.

*The struggle in
every moment*

Consecration

Most loving and all-powerful Father, you are the source of my hope and my joy.

1. *"All that is mine is yours."*

"Ask and you will receive."

Father, I firmly believe that your love is infinite.
  How could the love of your children
    vie with yours?
  Oh! The immensity of your fatherly love!
  All that is yours is mine.
  You counseled me to pray with sincerity,
  and I entrust myself to you, Father,
    full of goodness.

2. *"All is grace."*

"Your Father knows what you need."

Father, I firmly believe that from the beginning
  you provided everything for my greatest good.
  You never cease guiding my life.
  You accompany each of my steps.
  What could I fear?
  Prostrate before you, I adore your holy will.
  I put myself entirely into your hands,
  knowing that all things come about through you.
  I am your child; I believe that everything is grace.

3. *"I can do all things through Christ who strengthens me."*

"To the praise of his glory."

Father, I firmly believe that nothing
  surpasses the omnipotence
    of your Providence.
  Your love is infinite.
  I want to accept everything with a joyful heart:
  Praise and eternal thanksgiving,
  united to the Virgin Mary, St. Joseph,
    and the angels.
  I join my voice to those of people of all nations,
  to sing the glory of God,
  forever and ever. Amen.

4. *"Do all for the glory of God."*

"Your will be done."

Father, I firmly believe without hesitation,
  that you work and act in me.
  I am the object of your affection and tenderness.
  I ask you to realize in me
  all that can bring you greater glory.
  I ask only for your glory,
  that is enough to satisfy me
    and to make me happy;
  this is my greatest aspiration,
  the most urgent desire of my soul.

5. *"All for the mission! All for the Church!"*

Father, I firmly believe
  that you have entrusted me with a mission,
  engraved entirely with your love.

You prepare the way for me.
I will not cease readying myself,
and being firm in my resolution.
Yes, I have resolved
to become a silent offering.
I shall serve as an instrument
in the Father's hands.
I will offer my sacrifice,
moment by moment,
through my love for the Church.
"Here I am, I am ready!"

6. *"With fervent desire I have desired to eat this Passover with you."*

"It is consummated."

My beloved Father!
United to the sacrifice
of the Eucharistic celebration,
which I do not cease to offer,
I kneel at this moment
and speak this word
that comes from my heart: "Sacrifice."
A sacrifice that accepts humiliation
as well as glory,
a joyful and complete sacrifice
that sings of my hope and of all my love.

Cf. Lk 15:31; Mt 7:7; Mt 6:8; Phil 4:13; Eph 1:6;
1 Cor 10:31; Mt 6:10; Lk 22:15; Jn 19:30

The Redeemer

Jesus as Redeemer is a title Pope John Paul II has used in many of the most important writings of his pontificate:

Redemptor hominis: The Redeemer of Man;

Redemptoris mater: Mother of the Redeemer;

Redemptionis donum: The Gift of the Redemption.

Far from being a mere coincidence, the pope's stress on the Redeemer is born of his conviction and profound interior vision. The presence of the Redeemer has transformed the whole earth and all of human history in the admirable restoration of the dignity of the human person and our status as children of God.

ℒ 33 ℚ

Purification of the heart

All religions have some type of rite for purification, and those who want to purify themselves must go through them. The Jews purified themselves through the blood of sacrificial lambs or by plunging into the waters of the Jordan. Hindus bathe in the waters of the Ganges.

In the Gospel of Luke, we read something quite different: Jesus says that it is not enough to wash oneself in order to becomes pure. One must also purify one's interior dispositions. Those who listened to him had never heard such a teaching and were astonished, even offended by it.

And yet, Christ said unambiguously: *"Not what goes into the mouth defiles, but what comes out of the mouth, this is what defiles,"* and with even greater realism, he taught: *"The best way to purify a cup and a plate is to give what they contain to the poor."* This simple recommendation contains a remarkable truth: "It is in sharing one's goods with the poor that one is purified."

If I am still soiled, it is not because I have forgotten to perform some exterior rite—that would only be a form of superstition. It is because I lack righteousness and love for my neighbor that I remain impure. My stain comes from my heart, which no exterior rite can cleanse.

True purity consists in knowing how to share with one's brothers and sisters, and in knowing how to give. Mary, help me to understand this and to put it into practice! At times, I act as if I could elude God's gaze by hiding behind my exterior practices.

Am I a victim of a devotion to exterior rites, a disciple of empty practices? Do I underestimate the importance of the interior life?

Cf. Mt 15:11; Lk 11:37–41

*Purification
of the heart*

ℒ 34 ℒ

Purification for transformation

If I felt satisfied with the act of exterior purification alone, I would only be a disciple attached to forms and rites in themselves. Yet, purification has a more profound, interior meaning.

For an authentic disciple of Christ, *purification* means *transformation*—the transformation of my objective in view of which I use material goods, the transformation of my existence into a living offering to the Lord, and a precious gift for my brothers and sisters.

Purification transforms present situations or behaviors and orients them toward a new life. It implies certain demands and sacrifices that are more difficult than a simple washing of one's hands. Of what use are external ablutions if my inner life remains unchanged?

Water only cleans the surface; love purifies my heart. The flame of love will consume the impurities of my soul; without love, my will remains tarnished by pride, egoism, self-love, animosity, and greed. Can water get to the source of such stains? No. On the contrary, it makes them more harmful because we may try to hide behind or camouflage sinfulness under the appearance of ritualism and virtue. Thus, many people are unwittingly drawn to superficiality—including those who, like me, may continue to mistakenly think that they are already pure.

🖎 35 🖎

The Lord sees the heart

If I am still not a saint, it is because my way of looking at things is so different from yours, Lord. When a
sinner is not reconciled with you, Lord, you nevertheless
continue to love and call that sinner to repentance. When
a sinner repents and comes back to the Father's house,
you look on him or her as an entirely new person—as if
nothing had ever happened. When the converted sinner
lives in your peace, you forget everything, Lord. You have
cleansed everything in your blood and nothing remains
of the past. Henceforth, there exists only communion,
esteem, and trust.

I listen to you, Lord, when you tell me:

"Forget your brothers and sisters' past.
    If you base your relationships on the past
    then who will be mistaken: you or them?
    You will be the one in the wrong
    for not having forgiven.

"You want to know everyone's *'curriculum vitae,'*
    and that is why, little by little,
    communion is broken.

"I want to open the door wide to them,
    but you insist on keeping it closed.
    I want to forgive them,
    but you insist on condemning them.
    How different my way of seeing is from yours!

> *'Rejoice, because your brother was dead.*
> *Now he is alive.'"*

Lord, I can never exhaust the meaning
of these words.
I can only kneel before you and thank you
for your love.
Lord, I am not worthy to be called your child;
I see things so differently than you.

Cf. Lk 15:31–32

The Lord sees
the heart

A collaborator of love

Lord, I wanted to love you
   with all of my strength,
   not with my feelings alone
   but with my actions,
   not just at times,
   but continuously.

At first, this kind of love seemed difficult for me, but gradually I discovered that, even so, it was not impossible. What I needed was to raise my relationships to a supernatural level.

Everyone, from politician to farmer, is devoted to tasks, which affect others in one way or another. Their tasks either bring joy and satisfaction to others or pain, irritation, sadness.

Every word, gesture, glance, or greeting has its particular meaning, but one not defined in a dictionary. Words and gestures come from a person's heart with nuances of feeling unique to the individual. Two people may use the same words and gestures, but the meaning behind them makes all the difference. We must purify and become continually aware of our interior intentions.

How do I transform my intentions? Christ revealed this when he said: "*You did it to me.*" What I do for a relative or for someone I love might be entirely different from what I do for a stranger. But as a collaborator of love, I do everything to Jesus, my beloved Lord.

Here is an easy formula to remember: *"Others = Jesus"*
Applying this equation in my own life would make me a
collaborator of love forever.

Cf. Mt 25:40

A collaborator
  of love

ℒ 37 ℒ

The most effective means

I am inclined to seek new means to bear witness to God, means adapted to modern science and techniques like the radio, television, and the press. Generally, these means cost a great deal and I cannot afford to use them every day. But I tend to feel that without these means I am not an effective witness. Thus, I often overlook the most powerful and remarkable means of all: love.

Why place so much confidence in the efficacy of love? Because Jesus declared: *"By this all will know that you are my disciples, if you have love for one another."* Further, he made love the sole condition of his testament: *"My commandment is that you love one another."*

Perhaps there are more sophisticated means in the world than those at my disposal, but so often they do not bear witness to God because they are devoid of love.

From now on, Lord,
   help me to bring your love everywhere:
   to schools and hospitals,
   to marketplaces and theaters,
   to press and television.
   No one should be deprived
   of the environment of love.

Lord, love is the means you want me to use
   to bear witness to you,
   or you would have shown me another way.

Cf. Jn 13:34–35; Jn 15:12

A spirit of division

Divisions in the Church are the surest way to limit the spread of the Gospel. In his letter to Titus, St. Paul teaches that the community of Christ has the atmosphere of a common home where all differences are accepted. Each person finds a place there and all together the members struggle for the unity of humankind. Special clans or class distinctions do not exist, nor is there an attempt to construct communities that are closed in upon themselves and where those not "of our own group" do not find a place.

Lord, make me live in sincerity with myself.
Deliver me from hypocritical virtue
and from a sectarian spirit.
Help me not to construct
fortresses or blockhouses
where I only admit my "disciples,"
thus condemning innumerable others,
with their many abilities and gifts,
to languish, become poor, and despair.
They do not find their place in the Church
because of my authoritarianism,
and their only "fault"
is not belonging to the same neighborhood,
or not sharing the same background,
or not belonging to my spiritual family
or to my "club."

The knights of our time

In Medieval times, knights dedicated their lives to preserving their honor, protecting widows and orphans, and to defending their homeland.

Today, our "knights" combat injustice, oppression, racial discrimination, and dictatorships. They struggle to eradicate disease, famine, misery, illiteracy, and unemployment. In their peaceful efforts, they accept sacrifices in order to help build up a new economic system and to establish permanent harmony among nations. They dedicate themselves to science in the service of humanity.

These knights of love do not hesitate to go wherever the excluded, the sick, the hungry, those who hunger for truth, and those who thirst for tenderness need them.

There are people who may wear the trappings and bear the "name" of knight, but do not possess the heart of one. There are people who wear simple clothes and bear ordinary names, who truly have knightly hearts. They work positively, quietly—they need no exceptional gifts or money for this. I am called to the ranks of these "true knights."

Flame bearers

Jesus proclaimed that he had come to bring fire to the earth.

By continuing his mission, I keep alive the flame that my hands received from Christ Jesus. Just as a runner descends Mount Olympus carrying the Olympic torch, I want to traverse the entire world in order to transmit the flame of Christ to others.

The flame I bear is love, the élan of fervor, the strength of God, destined to inflame and consume sin and to renew all things.

But am I really a burning flame or an icy wind? Am I a stove without a flame? If that is what I am, then I am useless!

To feed this fire I must pour the oil of my daily prayer into others. I will prepare their torches so that the Holy Spirit will set them ablaze, dispelling their darkness and *"renewing the face of the earth."*

ℒ 41 ℒ

Complaints and criticisms

Criticism is easy; it is within everyone's reach. A pessimistic nature easily finds the defects and shortcomings in others. But everyone, without exception, has defects. Even the saints needed a lifetime to become Christ-like, to become perfect *"as our heavenly Father is perfect."*

Keeping an account of people's faults is a fruitless task. Not only are you showing your pride and ill will, but you are also wasting your time.

To remember a person's defects is to hold onto the past and to concentrate on that person's worst side, as if no other existed! No one's life is frozen; everyone is constantly evolving, changing, growing. You must concentrate your entire attention on the present and the future rather than the past.

One who has sinned, but who bears his or her past with sorrow may be a saint today or will become one tomorrow. Such a person may make swifter progress on the road toward holiness than me. While I waste my time and strength criticizing and complaining about others, those who seemed to me to be further behind on the road are setting out and moving forward quickly and soon will have gone beyond me.

Cf. Mt 5:48

❧ 42 ❧

The most splendid revolution

To protect our own ideas and beliefs, we sometimes surround ourselves with a protective barrier of barbed or electric wire and cement walls. And yet, despite the height and strength of our barriers, someone is always trying to climb over and the day will come when our walls will crumble.

My deeply rooted mental constructions, ideas, and habits are my worst enemies because they paralyze me from within. A revolution is necessary to free me from them. This revolution will demand many sacrifices of me, above all, the sacrifice of detaching myself from what seems important to me. It is at the price of this revolution that I will be liberated.

Before committing myself to this struggle, I must reflect carefully on each detail in order to detect lacunae, to be prepared to face the unexpected, and to be convinced of the validity of my choice. With skill and courage, and without regret, I will make the necessary sacrifices, because I am fighting for my freedom.

Your sacrifices, Lord Jesus, were unlimited!
You accepted misunderstanding
and others considering you insane.
In the eyes of the world, your defeat on the cross
was the most difficult possible.
You did not come to abolish the Law,
but to bring it to fulfillment

through the spirit of the Gospel.
Your teaching constitutes the treasure
  of Revelation,
the most splendid revolution.
You left me a new alliance sealed with your blood.
If I want to take part in your revolution,
my life must also be written in letters of blood.

The most
splendid
revolution

ℒ 43 ℒ

The Lord will not abandon me

Infinitely good Lord,
    you know my heart and my weaknesses.
    Do not abandon me.
    You are infinitely just
    and ask nothing of me
    that is beyond my strength.
    My happiness knows no limit
    when I contemplate your infinite righteousness
    and put all things in your hands.
    From experience I know that on my path,
    covered with innumerable obstacles,
    in the night of trial without exit,
    you, the infinitely righteous One
    have never abandoned me.

At those moments when I nearly fainted
    under the weight of evil,
    you did not abandon me.
    When I felt tempted to despair
    and to give up everything,
    when the storm raged without and within,
    when the winds of calumny buffeted
    against my good intentions and actions,
    Lord, you did not abandon me.

It was at such moments
    that the Holy Spirit taught me what I should do
    and how I should speak.

At such moments the Holy Spirit
poured courage and hope into my weakened soul
and comforted me.
The Lord will never abandon me
to my limitations!

Cf. Lk 12:11–12

*The Lord
will not
abandon me*

ℒ 44 ℒ

False gods

Even if religion is not opposed or persecuted in our times, there is nevertheless an indifference regarding it. It seems that religion has been substituted by the pursuit of material goods. Night and day, people run after gratification, material possessions, luxury, and a life of ease.

The goods God has given to us are a means for happiness in this world and of serving others. However, many people place an absolute value on material goods and invest all of their resources and energy into possessing them. Material goods become their idols—the gods that dominate their existence. Yet, Jesus warned: *"You fool! This night your soul will be required of you."* Woe to us who adore the false gods of our times!

Jesus did not address this warning only to dishonest merchants who are avid for gain and self-gratification, but to all of us, and above all to those consecrated to the Lord.

When an individual or a community gives such importance to money and material goods that these become the principal criterion of their success, leading them to vie for comfort and power, the Lord will say to them, *"You fool! This night your soul will be required of you."*

Cf. Lk 12:20

ℒ 45 ℒ

The use of this world's goods

Lord, you never prohibited the use of material goods. Why would you have created them if not for us to use and offer thanks to you, their Creator? Why should your children not make use of material goods and enjoy them? You did not teach us to deprive ourselves of the right to enjoy the gifts of this world. Rather, you taught us that a person's life and happiness are not to be bought or sold.

The core of the message revealed by Jesus is the value of the kingdom of heaven, this most precious of all wealth. You have taught me that there are two ways to appreciate the gifts of the world and wealth:

1. If my heart is closed, material wealth makes me a cog in the huge, complex machinery of greed. Then this word, *"You fool! This night your soul will be required of you"* refers to me. I thought myself rich, that I lacked nothing, but in reality, I am miserable and stripped of everything before the Lord.

2. On the other hand, if I open my heart wide to the Gospel, love will fill me entirely and with it the hope of the kingdom. I will be generous with others and filled with riches before you, Lord.

What place do material possessions have in my life? Is money my master or my servant? Do I have everything I could wish for, or am I deprived of what is important in the presence of God?

Cf. Lk 12:20

ℒ 46 ℒ

Is it easy to live with Jesus?

Living with Jesus. What an exhilarating prospect! It would be the same experience that Mary, Joseph, and the apostles lived. Jesus is meek and humble of heart, rich in mercy, the Holy One par excellence in whom all virtues dwell.

Yet, it is not always easy to live with saints. Even life with Christ is sometimes disconcerting to the human intelligence. Indeed, it implies a total change of self—the meaning of which is part of the Christian mystery.

God's presence in Jesus surpasses all human comprehension. Mary and Joseph must have realized how little they really understood Jesus and how far beyond them was the truth about their Son. How often they must have wondered:

How can our Son have a Father in heaven?
   Why does he answer his Father's call?
   Why does he say that the Temple is his house?
   Why did he not stay within the safety
      of his family?
   How did he come from the depths
      of the Divine mystery?
   Why is our child, who is God, so poor?
   Why does he work? Why must he die?
   And we, his parents, must share
      in his impoverished destiny.

Lord, you are infinitely good.
    You are humble.
    You are holy.
    You are generous in your forgiveness.
    And I am a miserable sinner,
    proud and full of spite.
    Only when I truly repent and change,
    will I realize that life with you
    is paradise.

*Is it easy
to live with
Jesus?*

The importance of time

It seems to me that different moments in our human existence make us either more objective or subjective depending on each circumstance. Indeed, time does not always carry the same weight. When we are happy, we want to prevent the hours from ever passing. When we are near a dying person, we want the hours to go slowly so we can be near that person for as long as possible. When we are suffering, it seems that the hours stand still and never end. We are ready to welcome whatever comes to us in times of joy, love, and intimacy.

Lord, I want to live each moment
    by filling it with my love,
    living each moment with the greatest intensity,
    just as the saints in heaven live their eternity.
    Each of their moments is made of love
    and their eternity is a beatitude
    that no tongue can ever describe.
    I must always live more intensely
    the time I have left.
    What counts is not so much how long I live,
    but how I lived the time I had.
    You will not question me about the number
      of years,
    but about the weight of the love
    reaped every day of my existence.

Remain in me

In chapter 15 of St. John's Gospel, I have noted the many times the verb *manere,* to remain, appears. When this verb is used, it indicates Jesus' strong insistence, profound emotion, and ardent desire. It signals an element of great importance in his teaching, a point that Jesus wants to engrave on the hearts of his disciples.

In Christ's time, as in our own, people were motivated by exterior feelings and distracted from the treasure of their interior life.

"Remain in me" is a simple, informal expression that reveals a desire for communion in love.

"Remain in me" goes beyond human comprehension; two people can only stay *near* one another, but how can they be *within* each other?

"Remain in me" is a form of permanent communion, which can be compared in some way to the effects of Eucharistic communion. I cannot receive the Eucharist as often as I wish during the day, but I can remain forever in you, Lord. You will be in me and I in you!

"To remain in you" is not an idle or passive love for God, rather it is active: *"He who remains in me, and I in him, will bear much fruit."*

Lord Jesus, I want to remain in you.
  You and I will be one:
  one unique will, one sole heart,
  one effort, one love.

Their will no longer be a distinction
between what belongs to you
and what belongs to me.

"It is no longer I who live, but Christ who lives in me."

Cf. Jn 15:5; Gal 2:20

*Remain
in me*

ℒ 49 ℒ

Preaching and silence

Lord, you have called me to preach the Gospel, but at the same time you invite me to solitude, silence, and prayer. How can these two great vocations be reconciled? At first glance, they seem to be so contradictory, but one who proclaims the Gospel preaches while remaining a person of prayer.

I will place all of my gifts into preaching the Gospel. *"Woe is me if I do not preach."* But when I am preaching, I want to remain in a continuous interior silence, allowing the Holy Spirit to speak to me and through me.

Silence is not a lack of effort but a time of prayer and preparation, reflection and maturation. Silence supplies me with the energy I need to proclaim the Gospel.

If, when I preach the Gospel, it makes no impact, perhaps it is because I have not allowed the Holy Spirit to speak.

In the twelve years of his missionary life, St. Francis Xavier traveled 80,000 kilometers—without car or plane—over mountains and across plains to preach the Gospel. And at night, he prayed alone in silence before the Holy Eucharist.

Cf. 1 Cor 9:16

ℒ 50 ℒ

Three conditions for renunciation

Jesus has three requirements for those who wish to follow him and become his disciples:

— renunciation of family;

— abandonment of all property;

— and the obligation to *"Take up your cross...."*

I find many ambiguities when I read these phrases from the Gospel:

"If anyone comes to me and does not hate his father and mother, wife and children...he cannot be my disciple."

"Whoever does not bear his cross and come after me cannot be my disciple."

"Whoever of you does not forsake all that he has cannot be my disciple."

Lord Jesus, why do you oblige me to hate those who are so dear to me? And surely, the goods of this world are not so evil; they are sometimes very necessary! Why renounce them? And yet, you make these the heart of your message. Lord, help me to understand. Teach me!

Those who follow must go beyond the narrow limits of race, nationality, family, and egotism, and work for the good of the entire human community.

Those who follow me have left everything, and their sole aim is to serve the kingdom.

Those who follow me use everything to the advantage of their brothers and sisters, without saving anything as security for themselves.

Thus, your followers gain everything! When my heart, like the heart of the Virgin Mary, is completely empty, it will then be filled with God.

Cf. Lk 14:27; Lk 14:26; Lk l4:33

*Three
conditions for
renunciation*

ℒ 51 ℒ

The false gospel

In his letter to the Corinthians, St. Paul speaks of *"another Gospel"* different from the one he proclaimed. There is a false gospel, which differs from the true one. How can we distinguish between them? We must observe the difference in the lives of those who serve one gospel rather than the other—looking for the signs of false righteousness, false freedom, and false virtue.

In order to be able to distinguish between the true and the false, I myself must be entirely evangelized for fear that the Gospel message within me is insufficient or that my life is not yet authentically gospel-oriented.

First I must be permeated with the Gospel, and then help it to permeate others and today's society. Only in this way will I help to build up a renewed people in a renewed society. I must not be satisfied with living virtuously for myself alone, I must commit myself to living virtuously in today's world. This is a responsibility and some day I will have to give an account of it to the Lord, who will ask, "Did you consume your strength so as to alleviate sufferings, or were you indifferent to them?"

I love to meditate on this phrase from the Gospel: *"I am the vine, you are the branches."* When we allow ourselves to be infused by the life-giving sap of the Gospel, we will be completely renewed and we will *be* the true Gospel, because we will be filled with the Lord Jesus.

Cf. 1 Cor 11:4; Jn 15:5

Prisons

The world is now fully aware of the unspeakable horrors of concentration camps such as Dachau and Auschwitz, which are situated in historic reality, in specific geographic locations, and as a shadow in the human memory.

Today there are new Dachaus and Auschwitzes. In new camps, whether known or unknown, visible or hidden, victims of injustice and oppression are confined. Only attentive observers are aware of their existence. Yes, concentration camps still exist, enclosed behind the barbed wire of injustice and raised by those who oppress and despoil. But my indifference also helps to build these enclosures!

Each day so many of my brothers and sisters of Asia, Africa, Latin America, Vietnam, China, Cuba, and Iran walk the way of their passion and climb their Calvary. They are Jesus, abandoned, forgotten, and rejected by cruelty and injustice.

Because I am afraid of soiling my hands, of compromising myself, because I do not want to give up my comforts, well-being, and gratification, I try to forget them, to not think of them any more…. But their reality is ever present and weighs heavily on my conscience.

Lord, give me the courage
    to break down the enclosures
    of selfishness, cowardice,

discrimination, and greed
that encircle the world and hold it prisoner.
And forgive me for my contribution
in building up prisons of injustice and
    oppression.

Prisons

✥ 53 ✥

Christ's sacrifice continues

In a mysterious but real way Jesus never ceases to offer his sacrifice in the Eucharistic celebration.

But it is not enough to celebrate the Eucharist strictly according to liturgical rites. Christ offers his sacrifice with immense fervor, as in the hour of his passion and crucifixion, when he obeyed the Father even to the point of his humiliating death on the cross—a sentence reserved for slaves and common criminals. Then, Jesus felt abandoned, even by his Father.

Grant, Lord, that we may offer
    the Eucharistic sacrifice with great love.
If we do not offer ourselves with Jesus in some way:
    if our lives are safe from hunger, thirst, cold,
        and humiliation;
    if our faces are not struck by slaps and spittle;
    if a crown of thorns is not inflicted upon us;
    if we do not carry the cross,
    are not nailed to it,
    do not die on it;
    and if we are not buried in another's tomb,
    then we must be transformed.
    If because of fear I try to escape Jesus' destiny,
    then despite all the rites I follow
    and all their solemnity,
    I am not offering the Eucharistic sacrifice
    with Jesus' sentiments.

🙋 54 🙋

Broken communion

Love calls us to union and union calls us to communion. Why is this communion so often broken?

I had the opportunity to visit many Gothic churches in Paris, Rheims, Chartres, and Cologne. Everywhere I was told, "This building is slowly deteriorating and will have to be repaired, holes filled in, and stones replaced." The pollution in the atmosphere attacks even stone! Communion can be destroyed in the same way.

> The atmosphere of communion is polluted
>> when I egotistically seek my own interests
>> and not those of my brothers and sisters,
>> and those of the Lord;
>> when I oblige others to follow my will
>>   and not God's;
>> when I take back what I already offered
>>   with generosity;
>> when I judge my brothers and sisters unjustly;
>> and when I lock them into their deficiencies.
>
> Lord Jesus, we are in communion
>> when you are among us,
>> because you bring your life into ours.
>> When we go away from you,
>> we also abandon our brothers and sisters,
>> and communion is broken.

If I substitute your presence, Lord,
   with selfishness, prejudice, self-love, jealousy...
   I put love to death
   and communion is broken.
   The only true communion is in you, Lord.

Broken
communion

The influence of a saint

What possible benefit does society gain from the existence of a saint in its midst? A saint may not be an inventor of new products or machinery that contributes to humanity's advancement, but the advantages that person brings to the Church and society are anything but negligible.

However far away his or her hermitage may be, people seek out saints. The saint indicates the way that leads to God, incessantly proclaims the Gospel, and awakens faith in others. The holiness of the saintly person shines like the light of the silent stars in the vault of the heavens. The life, example, and teachings of the saint cross over centuries. A saint is also a "savior" through whom God manifests his mercy. The saint assists the miserable and those who have sinned and brings reconciliation, peace, and love to the world.

Whereas a person attached to sin can bring division and contributes to that which harms the world, the person attached to a holy life can bring the Word of God and contributes to the life of humanity. The Lord lives and acts through saints and nothing stands in the way of the power of Divine grace.

Lord, give to our world many saints.
I may produce material goods,
but you alone, Lord, can give us saints.

Do not abandon your responsibility

I desire to remain firmly at my post!
   How could I abandon it?
   Those who forsake their responsibility
   are often cowards or egotists,
   cunning mercenaries,
   seeking their own profit.
Despite the difficulty
   and the danger involved,
   I will not yield an inch of ground!
   I will not take one step backward.
   I will remain firm even at the risk of my life...
   I would rather let the enemy walk over my body
   than abandon my responsibility!

The Christian is a front line soldier.

"Behold, we are going up to Jerusalem, and the Son of Man will be betrayed to the chief priests and to the scribes."

"Shall I not drink the cup which my Father has given me?"

"That the world may know that I love the Father, and as the Father gave me commandment, so I do. Arise, let us go from here."

I will stay at my post,
   not as a soldier
   who only seeks security for self

while allowing others to bear suffering
    and isolation.
Lord, free me from such wisdom,
which is not a gift of the Holy Spirit.

Cf. Mt 20:18; Jn 18:11; Jn 14:31

*Do not
abandon your
responsibility*

༄ 57 ༄

My will or yours?

Faith teaches me that I am permanently bound to God, my Father, and that my existence does not depend on me or on my decisions. In reality, however, we often establish lifetime projects and make decisions for our Father, so to speak, as did the Prodigal Son—and with evident results: disappointment and self-reproach. The life projects we established with human intelligence alone do not satisfy us.

If we renounce our status as children of God because we do not want to accept God's teaching, we will lose our peace of soul.

Lord, grant me the strength to return to you,
   like the prodigal son.
   You are the principle of my life
   and no one knows as well as you
   what is most useful for me.
   You have traced a path for each of us
   in the plan of your love.
   At each instant, we want to offer you our will.
   In spite of ourselves,
   we will not merely be resigned,
   but as your children will be always available
     to your plan for us.
   May your will be ours!

The mystery of grace

Jesus' message is contained entirely in these two elements: grace and response.

To be a Christian, I must listen to God's Word; my heart must be completely open to grace and to receiving the love that God grants me through Jesus.

When I live this mystery of God's love, the Lord communicates new life to me. This new life is not based in a relationship according to the flesh; God roots my new family in the kingdom of heaven.

Whoever listens to the Word of God and lives it, belongs to this community of Jesus and Mary. There we find communion and reciprocal confidence.

This new life has its demands. The barriers erected by society, which separate people based on social conditions, political ideas, and religious beliefs must be broken down.

The authentic Christian receives God's love as the guiding principle that transforms the individual into an artisan of peace among all people.

Only the person who responds by putting God's word into practice and desires to live it wholly can claim to have truly listened to it.

Cf. Lk 8:19–21

Prayer opens the heart to God's love

Lord Jesus, you have taught me to pray with confidence and to prepare my heart to receive the Father's love..."*Your kingdom come, Your will be done,*" to have the same confidence in the Father's word as the man who awakened his friend in the middle of the night, or as the son who asked his father for a fish.

The more I meditate on Christian prayer, the more I find that it is essentially a preparation to receive God's grace and the kingdom which is coming.

When my prayer is sincere, I ardently desire the coming of the Lord and I receive the Holy Spirit—that most sublime gift of the Father.

The gift of the Father's love is the kingdom of heaven and to receive the kingdom is to be forgiven, on the condition that we know how to forgive our own brothers and sisters. In praying the *Our Father,* I discover that to love God is to become conscious of God's love for us. For this reason, I must be ready to receive God's love. I need only cry out, *"Father!" (Abba).* And in the silence, I will hear my Father answering: *"Your Father in heaven will give the Holy Spirit to those who ask him for it."*

Several times a day, in the name of the Lord Jesus, I will send up my cry: *"Father!"* Then the Holy Spirit will help me to understand everything.

Cf. Lk 11:5–8; 11:11–12; 11:4; 11:13

ℒ 60 ℒ

God loves without limit

Lord, you desire your love to be expressed through my life and in my relationships with others. Kneeling before you, I examine myself and see that I have sometimes lived as a man absorbed in the details of the law. At times, I have been a hypocrite. While my daily life seemed correct, even virtuous, this appearance only masked an interior void.

I feel I deserve your stern warning: *"Woe to you..."* I have concentrated my attention on the unimportant details and exterior aspects of virtue. I was harsh with others and closed to your goodness. My behavior was in conflict with the advice I gave others, with my teaching, and my statements.

I have lived as if separated from your commandments, but made a heavy burden of them for others to bear. I required their observance of the minutest iota, and distorted religion to the point that I made it detestable to others. I transformed your image into that of a judge or police officer. Instead, Lord, you are all good, and you love without limit. *"Come unto me all you who labor and are heavy laden, and I will give you rest."*

Cf. Lk 11:42–46; Mt 11:28

An apostle of Mary

Soul of Mary,
   sanctify me in the Holy Spirit!
   Body of Mary, keep me in your womb
   with the Lord Jesus
   in one interior life!
   Blood of Mary, flow within me
   as your blood flowed in Jesus.
   Transform me into your spirit, O Mary.
   May you nourish me
   as you nourished the infant Jesus,
   with food enriched by your virtues!

May I be loved by your most loving heart,
   as you loved Jesus.
   Give me your love, Mary,
   so that I can love all people
   and accept all the risks
   involved in the adventure for God's kingdom.

Tears of Mary, purify me from my faults
   and of the complicities which sadden Jesus' heart.
   From cowardice, laziness,
   and from the wisdom of this age,
   preserve me, O Mother!

May your words of life teach me
   to understand and to love Jesus,
   to speak of him, to unite myself to him,
   to become his word in the world.

May your sweet gaze illuminate me
so that I may know the world in its truth,
and discover in it the signs of the times.
The sweetness of your look, Mary,
is my consolation and my strength,
a reminder of your motherly presence.

May your provident hand guide me
as you guided Jesus on the path
prepared by the Father, which led to Calvary.
As you accompanied Jesus
at every moment of his earthly life,
accompany me with your light step
during my apostolic tasks,
    even the most common.

May your sufferings strengthen me, Mary,
and all witnesses of Jesus,
so that the Father's will may be accomplished
in the redemption.

May your unfailing presence
keep me faithful at every instant,
in an offering to your heart
that makes me a living *Ave*.
Through your hands, Mary,
I offer my entire life to Jesus, and to Joseph;
I want to accept everything for love of you.

O Mary, my Mother, our Mother,
Mother of the Church,
with you I will work for the salvation
    of all people.

With you, I will overcome every difficulty
and trial
for the Church, the work of your Son,
so that it may be one.
I entrust you with my past,
my present, and my future;
with my sins, my desires, and my destiny
as well as the destiny of those I love.
As Joseph's work was also yours,
may my tasks be yours.
It is in you that I live, hope,
and pray without ceasing,
in union with the Holy Trinity.
Like you, I want to become love,
and to carry your presence everywhere
so as to build an ever more beautiful world,
as Jesus desires,
in which people love one another
and live happily and in peace.
I ask you, O Mary, to give me a heart
that loves you more each day.
May all people love you,
follow your example,
and share their pain, waiting, worries,
struggles, and joys with you
for the kingdom of heaven.
Mary, my Mother,
for all my life and for all eternity
I will thank you for being *our Mother,*

for having given Jesus to us,
for having chosen me as a priest
     and apostle of your heart.
Mary, my Mother, my only hope,
my first love, my portion,
as you participated in the sacrifice
at the foot of the cross,
stay close to me each day,
especially at the hour of my last sacrifice.
In Paradise, receive me as the good thief,
your son, and the brother of Jesus.

O our Mother,
for me to live is Christ;
for me to live is Mary and Joseph.
For me to live is a continual renewal
in the spirit of the Second Vatican Council.
For me to live
is to collaborate in the evangelization
of the regions of the Pacific
with a view to the third millennium.

*An apostle
  of Mary*

The secret of success

In prison I am so often elsewhere in spirit, worried about the future of my country. How can my beloved country, now so wounded, be reconstructed? The task of reconstruction falls upon every individual, in every milieu, and particularly on workers.

Four words summarize what is necessary for a complete reconstruction of life: "Work, intelligence, union, and tradition." This is the secret of success; these four interdependent elements are essential and irreplaceable for anyone who is passionately in love with his or her own role in the world.

It is the call and the will of the Lord that we bring holiness to the environment in which we live and that we become holy ourselves.

Lord, help my brothers and sisters
    to become conscious of the importance
    of their role in the world,
    of knowing how to find light in your Word
    and strength in the Eucharist.
    If they wanted to,
    they could change the world.

Work

The value of work is not in the effort exerted or in the fruits of that effort. The human person is not a machine. Our greatness lies in exercising our gift of intelligence. Far from making us slaves, our work is a continuation of God's creation by making us participants in the work of God. Our work makes both nature and life more beautiful.

Lord, teach me the virtues of work:
    the patience of a sculptor modeling a statue,
    of a weaver making a blanket,
    or of a seamstress bent over fabric.
    Teach me the vivacity of a young person
      at a computer,
    the perseverance of a farmer in a field,
    the tenacity of a mechanic repairing a car,
    the dignity of a mother cooking for her family,
    the tenderness of a nurse.

If I cherish my occupation
    and respect those I serve and yet do not know,
    smiling and showing my satisfaction
    and joy from the depths of my heart,
    offering the fruit of my labor for others use,
    then all I do becomes my work,
    and my life will be a gift
    offered to the Lord through those I encounter.

✒ 64 ✒

Human intelligence

The more humanity advances in progress and civilization, the more we strive to make work less burdensome, to diminish the risks and fatigue involved, to augment its quality, and to better respond to expectations.

The exercise of intelligence in my work is an act of self-offering and charity, because I must serve my neighbor with all my faculties. I must exercise my mind in competition, not through a sense of envy, but through a desire to challenge and surpass myself each day.

To exercise my mind
so as to act intelligently and to develop initiative,
so as to reflect and to choose,
so as to study, analyze, and discover,
so as to learn from others
and to draw lessons for life from experience.

The exercise of the mind is not reserved for intellectuals and scientists or those in the business world. The Lord Jesus taught: *"You must love the Lord your God with all of your mind."*

For the glory of God
and the happiness of my brothers and sisters,
may all of my actions give praise to God.

Cf. Mt 22:37

Unity

Work can only bear fruit when it is done in solidarity with others. Gone is the era of the artisan who worked alone. In a world of computers, electronics, and mass production, people must work together and pool their intelligence.

We must join to fight injustice, oppression, and violence. We must join and pool our strength to fight against poverty, disease, and ignorance. We must join to give a unified direction to our actions.

> To join others, an individual must accept
> sacrifice and discipline.
> A person must accept a higher ideal,
> eliminate the tendency to dominate,
> and destroy egoism and a partisan spirit.

> Today, "union" is often dictated by special interests
> and the strength of particular groups,
> who frequently achieve their goal
> through international intrigue and maneuvers,
> which sometimes provoke fierce wars,
> and thus, destroys itself:

"A bad tree cannot produce good fruits."

> True union is possible only in the Holy Spirit.
> Jesus, who knows us in the depths of our being,
> prayed:
> *"That they all may be one, as you, Father, are in me
> and I in you."*

Cf. Mt 7:17; Jn 17:21

Tradition

Every nation, family, and profession has its traditions. Tradition can be strength for a nation, especially in times of danger. In the economic and commercial work-a-day world, success is associated with adherence to a certain company tradition—a tried and now familiar presentation of a product or service. A company or manufacturer may keep the same name for centuries. A traditional brand name on boxes of chocolate, containers of butter, or bottles of wine inspire confidence in the consumer, even as they are always updating their manufacturing techniques and the quality of their products.

The great makers of automobiles, such as Mercedes, Rolls Royce, Renault, Peugeot, Fiat, Ford, Honda, etc., never stop renewing their techniques, while keeping their original tradition.

I must adapt traditions to new realities, develop them based on today's scientific and technological contributions, and renew them according to the latest discoveries. At the same time, I must keep my originality and preserve my personal gifts.

As long as I respect tradition, I enjoy everyone's confidence.

Cultural tradition
   and Christian tradition
   incarnated in culture and in art.

Let go of the past

Roll up your sleeves and begin to work! This means we must be aware of our responsibility toward our brothers and sisters, accept our mission, and be determined to overcome evil. We must take up this task again and again.

However modestly, the sinful woman, Nicodemus, and Peter began again with courage, hope, and determination, making the second half of their lives more beautiful than the first.

Reconstruct and reinforce! This is a law of historical reality and apostolic action—even when everything crumbled, even after 300 years of Christian persecution under the Roman Empire! Linus, Cletus, Clement, and Sixtus succeeded Peter after his death. After Paul's death came Cyprian, Cornelius, and Chrysogonus. The generations followed one after another.

In my country of Vietnam, the same thing happened. The Trinh, the Tay Son, the Nguyen dynasties passed away, but the Church remained and our ancestors continued the work. When difficulties seemed to bring everything they had done to ruin, they began again with love and unshakeable trust in the Lord and in their brothers and sisters.

They did not waste time recalling their insufficiencies, defeats, and difficulties. The Lord is not looking for passive saints.

After the resurrection, Jesus did not return to the past, rather, in complete faith he turned toward the future: *"Go into all the world and preach the Gospel to every creature."*

Cf. Mk 16:15

Let go
of the past

ℓ 68 ℓ

To begin again

Subjecting my brothers and sisters to criticism for shortcomings while failing to raise a finger to help them shows how afraid I am of compromising myself and soiling my hands.

If I truly loved my brothers and sisters,
    and truly sought only God's glory,
    I would recognize my responsibility toward them,
    I would collaborate with them and offer
        to help them.
    I would roll up my sleeves and begin to work
        and to fight—
    and not just once!
    To vanquish the enemy,
        one must begin again often.

Begin again with perseverance
    to do better than the time before,
    to rebuild and reorganize.
    This is a principle of historical
        and apostolic reality.
    God created human beings in a marvelous way,
    but when humanity fell, despite our sin,
    God restored us in an even more marvelous way.

Peter, Paul, and the Christians of the early Church never stopped pursuing the goal. When necessary they began again, trusting in God's power and in the good will and strength of the human person.

In the Gospel, we read the many setbacks people experienced in their lives, but Jesus commands them to begin again right away:

"Go and sin no more."

"Go, sell what you have, and give to the poor...
then follow me."

After having put my hand to the plow I will not look back, I will look up at the horizon.

Cf. Mt 19:21; Jn 5:14

To begin
again

The dignity of women

When considering the call of women, some people think only of the vocation of motherhood. From antiquity, Oriental societies identified woman with a fertile womb; even modern Western societies often consider woman only in relation to her sensuality.

Jesus considered and treated women as human beings. And it is in the sublime setting of our humanity that the dignity and true happiness of men and women is realized. Very often, as is seen throughout Scripture and history, it is because of women that men are able to listen to God and to live the mystery of grace with its demands.

Mary, Mother of God,
   you are the model of faith for all of us—
   men and women.
   You are the representative of all humanity,
   because you welcomed the most sublime
      of all graces:
   the presence of God on earth.
   God's presence transforms all things,
   even if no exterior change is apparent.
   The most marvelous mystery
      in the history of humanity
   was accomplished through your offering
      and collaboration:
   "God became man."

For having believed, you are blessed
　　and worthy of praise.
　　Your existence is the fountain of joy and blessing
　　for all women and men who believe
　　as you believed.

*The dignity
of women*

By the working of the Holy Spirit

The Holy Spirit took total possession of you,
   Virgin Mary.
   The Spirit dwells in you, lives in you,
   and in you realizes the greatest work
      of human history:
   "The Word was made flesh..."
   The Holy Spirit acts freely in you;
   you belong to the Spirit,
   Mary, for me you are a model
   of obedience and docility,
   of faith and of abandonment to the Holy Spirit;
   "...by the working of the Holy Spirit."

Teach me to listen to the Holy Spirit: *"It is the Spirit of the Father who speaks in you."*

Teach me to entrust myself to the Holy Spirit: *"The Spirit himself makes intercession for us with groanings which cannot be uttered."*

Teach me to allow the Holy Spirit the freedom to act within me: *"For as many as are led by the Spirit of God, these are the children of God."*

The Holy Spirit is the soul of the Church,
   the strength of martyrs,
   the confidence of pastors,
   and the single-heartedness
      of consecrated persons.

The human mind cannot understand all of this. Meditation on the Word of God introduces us into this mystery. Only God can reveal to us what God's Spirit is and how powerful and sweet is the Spirit's action in our souls.

Come, O Holy Spirit!
Veni Creator Spiritus!

Cf. Jn 1:14; Mt 10:20; Rom 8:26; Rom 8:14

*By the
working of the
Holy Spirit*

Serving with all our strength

You have entrusted me with a mission, Lord, and you invite me to take responsibility by sharing in your redemptive work. Everything comes about through your infinite love. At the same time, everything also depends on my response. I must be conscious of the greatness of the mission entrusted to me, which is nothing less than Jesus' mission.

"As the Father has sent me, so I send you."

Lord, for me your name is Savior. I have consecrated all of my life for this mission: salvation. In your footsteps, I am "savior" for the people of the present time. Grant that my whole life may be penetrated by the greatness of this mission!

To fulfill my mission I must pray, be prepared, act, collaborate, and observe. Your example, Jesus, is always before me. You accomplished your mission on Calvary, sacrificing your life for it. Yes, the mission you have given me is worthy of all my strength and my entire life, because it involves the love of God and the love of my brothers and sisters.

> I must love with all my spirit
> with all my strength,
> with all of my soul,
> with all of myself.

Because what I do without passion is destined to fail,
   success depends on the absoluteness
      of my commitment.
   "All for my mission."

Once I have completed my mission, I will be at peace.
Lord, I entrust to you what has yet to be done. This is my
mission as well.

Cf. Jn 20:21

*Serving with
all our strength*

Mary's silence

Mary, you are the Mother of the Word Incarnate:
  the happiest of all human beings,
  because you spoke to the Word of God.
You are the Queen of the Apostles,
  and you spoke, reminding the apostles
    of Jesus' words
  and commenting on them.
But you are also the Mother of interior silence,
  because you listened to what the Word told you.
  You allowed the Holy Spirit to address you,
  and you were attentive to the teaching
    that your Son,
  the Word, gave to his apostles.
What you do, you do for the Church.
  No one is happier than you, Mary,
  because you are still closest
    to the Incarnate Word.
  No one is more silent than you, Mary,
  because you are most attentive
  in your nearness to the Incarnate Word.
Why is there so little silence in me?
  I am often far from the Word,
  because listening to the Word
  is not yet a habit,
  because I have not yet asked you, Mary,

to teach me to listen to Jesus,
and to listen to you, Mother of interior silence.

If I were to meet Jesus today,
I would listen to him without tiring.
I want to shout to all around me:
"Silence! Listen to the Lord who is speaking!"
Why do so many people have ears
and do not listen?
Perhaps because they are too far away
from the Word
to be able to hear him,
and they never stop listening to other voices.

The saints experienced
peace and interior silence
because they were so close to God.

*Mary's
silence*

That we may be one

Everyone has his or her own personality and this can make it very difficult to live together. But "difficult" does not mean "impossible," otherwise Jesus would never have prayed: *"That they all may be one!"*

What is essential is to have confidence
   in you, Lord,
  and to put myself to work,
  hand in hand with others to express friendship,
  shoulder to shoulder to bear the same burden,
  moving forward in step,
  united in a mutual encounter.

In the face of difficulties I will not break,
  I will imitate the rushes and reeds,
  each one leaning toward the other.
  Heart to heart—united in love,
  mind to mind—united in intelligence
  so as to be able to reflect together
   and find the truth.

On this path, we will reach communion.
  The Lord will welcome and share a meal with us.
  Not only did he pray for us:
  "Father, I pray that they may be one,"
  but he also asked the highest degree of union
  for us—and I ask for it with you, Lord:
"As you, Father are in me, and I in you."

Cf. Jn 17:21

⫷ 74 ⫸

A transparent vessel

"Woe unto you, lawyers! For you have taken away the key of knowledge. You did not enter in yourselves, and those who were entering you hindered."

Jesus addresses this warning to me: I must not manipulate God's truth. Some people are self-proclaimed owners of truth. They are the only ones who can understand and comment on God's law and word. They put the truth at the service of their personal interests, and whoever dares to upset their way of living transgresses God's law. Today, as yesterday, this is a danger that threatens the Church.

I must examine myself: am I transparent enough to allow the Lord's message to move through me and to be the faithful transmitter of the truth in every detail? Or do I deform the truth by altering its requirements, rewriting certain aspects, arranging it according to my own needs, warping, disguising, or blurring it—then embroidering an attractive design to cover my manipulation?

Lord,
 I want to be your faithful messenger
 with those who have suffered
  for bearing witness to you,
 with those who have been persecuted
 for having followed your way,
 the traditional destiny reserved for your prophets.

There are aspects of this world
   that shut the door to your message
   and refuse to let it in.
   The Christian drama continues...
   blessed are those who hear Jesus' message
   with a pure heart.

Cf. Lk 11:52

A
transparent
vessel

ℰ 75 ℒ

Service without conditions

To dwell in God is to be in the center;
   everything revolves around the Sun.
To dwell in God is to be in contact
    with all creation.
   If I move away from God, I lose everything.
   Why lament and worry?
   I will place everything in God's hands
   without fear and without conditions.
   It is useless to add "ifs," "buts," "hows," or "whys"
   to my resolution to serve.

It is useless to say, "I am ready to accomplish this mission on the condition that I do not have to work with this person..." or, "I will leave my present assignment, but wherever I am sent, I must have...".

There must be no conditions
   in the Lord's service and work.
   Even when Mary asked, *"How can this be?"*
   she desired to be faithful to God.
   And the Lord answered her
   through the voice of the angel:
   "The Holy Spirit will come upon you."
   Mary immediately added:
   "Let it be done to me according to your word."
At that very instant
   she entered the stable of Bethlehem,

lived the flight into Egypt,
dwelt in the workshop of Nazareth,
and stood at the foot of the cross.

Cf. Lk 1:34, 38

*Service
without
conditions*

℘ 76 ℘

How can we become saints?

Lord, you have asked me, ignorant and sinful,
   to become holy as *"my Father who is in heaven."*
   In seeking this priority,
   the fundamental and essential means for holiness,
   I prayed that you would teach me simply
   how to become a saint.
   But your answer caused me to lose heart.
   Then I remembered your word:
   "I thank you, Father,
   that you have revealed these things to babes."

I see clearly that every saint
   has his or her particular "style,"
   no one of them resembles another.
   Each saint has his or her own way of holiness.

Yet, a common way exists that everyone,
   without exception, must undertake.
   "I must resemble the Lord Jesus."
   "I must do the will of him who sent me."
   "I have kept the commandments
     that the Father gave me."

This means that I must accomplish the tasks
   of the present moment, Lord,
   and respond to your grace at every instant,
   placing total confidence in you
   and leaving you free

to accomplish in me
your plan and not mine.
I must collaborate with all of my strength.
Thus, my specific role will assume its proper
splendor,
modestly but with the "necessary audacity"!
It was you, Lord Jesus, who told your apostles:
"You will do even greater works than these!"
Father, make me the littlest of all!

Mt 6:10; Mt 11:25; Jn 5:30; Jn 15:10; Jn 14:12

*How can
we become
saints?*

Love is confirmed by truth

Without the truth, love could not survive.
   In love, I want to see my brothers and sisters
   with God's eyes not with my own.

God sees my brothers and sisters
   much differently than I do.
   God sees the errors of their past,
   yet at the same time God's gaze
   embraces their sincere desire for conversion.
   How then can their past exist?

Our sincerity, repentance, and love
   are met by God's mercy.
   It is similar to the confidence a mother inspires
   in her fragile child as she lovingly
   protects it from the danger of falling.
   If my whole being is not full of mercy for others,
   I am not worthy to call myself a Christian.
   Without mercy, I cannot hope to receive
   the Lord's mercy.

"Blessed are the merciful,
   for they shall obtain mercy."

You have loved me, Lord,
   who created me from clay.
   You know my fragility and my weakness,
   and show me your tender mercy.

Cf. Mt 5:7

"The greatest success is holiness"

[John Paul II]

To be successful by the usual standards of the world means acquiring:

— power...while the saints relied on God's omnipotence;

— riches...while the saints enjoyed the Creator's abundant gifts;

— university degrees...while the saints shared in divine wisdom;

— admiration...while the saints rejoiced to be the objects of God's love.

Holiness is not the passive presence of God in a person, but God's life and action in that person. Holiness is a human life filled with God—the most beautiful life possible.

Holiness comes down through the centuries
without being degraded, or corrupted.
Holiness renders a person blessed.
Holiness truly transforms a person
and raises him or her to the highest level: God.
Holiness fills a person with love
and the Holy Spirit moves him or her.
Holiness is the most beautiful thing in the world.
If we gathered all the light of the sun into a person,

he or she would shine with splendor.
Yet, as unimaginable as this splendor is,
who can begin to speak of the beauty
of a soul in which God dwells?
The saint is "made" by the happy collaboration
of an individual with God, the author
    of all beauty.
Lord, I have only one lifetime to become holy!
    I know this requires openness and effort,
    because it is the highest of values.
    Holiness allows a person to show forth,
    like a vase of pure crystal,
    not merely a portrait of God,
        but God's true image.

"The
greatest success
is holiness"

What is a saint?

For someone to be canonized a saint there must be proof of the exercise of heroic virtue, which God confirms in miraculous ways.

I wish to humbly follow the example of the saints. I love the simple yet profound words of the poor peasant of Ars who was asked what he thought of his parish priest, St. John Vianney: "I saw God in a man," the peasant responded. Indeed, God so fills the life of a saint that God's presence shines forth from him or her. The Archangel's greeting to Mary on the day of the Annunciation offers us a definition of holiness: *"Hail Mary, full of grace"*—that is, *full of God.*

A saint is a person like any other; he or she has not been released from the daily human combat between virtue and sin, life and death. But when the saint fails, in humility he or she repents and asks God's pardon. The saint places all of his or her faith in God, even when faced with trials. In the saint's heart, now divested of those things that prevent attachment to God, the Lord pours peace, grace, and completeness. God lives in the saint, *"We will come to him, and make our home with him,"* and will use the saintly person in the plan of salvation.

The saints give themselves completely to the Lord Jesus, and the Lord gives himself completely to them.

How the saints used time

The saints lived on earth as much as I do.
  The saints were swept along
    by the same current of time.
  Their days were twenty-four hours long
  and not one minute more!
  All their lives were not longer in years:
  Francis Xavier died at the age of forty-six,
  Therese of the Child Jesus at twenty-four,
  and Rose of Lima at thirty-one.
  But the years they lived
  were incomparably intense and concentrated,
  because they recognized that time
    had the value of eternity.
God works through the saints
  who collaborate with God.
  How much we must esteem a single moment
  of the Lord's work!

We build holiness in the present moment not by turning to the past or anticipating the future. That is why the saints treasured the present moment; without neglecting a single instant, they made each moment a response of their whole being to God's love.

The saints lived in the present as in an immense ocean of peace because they already lived in that unending present of eternity.

To give life

The soul gives life to the body, and without the soul the body—whatever its size—is a corpse. A home or city without the strength of its inhabitants breathing "a soul," so to speak, into it, is also dead. Without such a soul, even a popular tourist site, regardless of its famous sights and spectacular monuments, remains a dead city.

Lord, my life, my activities,
   and the society in which I live
   must have a soul breathed into them.
   This is the work of the Holy Spirit.
   Am I animated by the Holy Spirit,
   the Spirit of Christ,
   or by the spirit of "the devil, the flesh,
     and the world"?
   To evangelize is to give life,
   and to let the wind of Pentecost
   renew the face of the earth.
   The Lord has sent me to proclaim
   the Good News to the poor.
   Thank you, Lord.

I fear for those who evangelize
   without the breath of the Holy Spirit,
   without the Virgin Mary, without the apostles,
   without the passion
     and the resurrection of Christ,
   for they cannot give the Word of life.

If it has been a long time
   since I led another to the faith,
   perhaps my preaching of the Gospel
   is not animated by the breath
      of the Holy Spirit.

To
give life

Pray always

Prayer is the breath of the soul.
  Without prayer, the soul suffocates.
Through prayer, I live in you, Lord.
  I live in you as a baby in its mother's womb
  with its breath united to hers
  and its heart beating in rhythm with hers...
Lord Jesus, you are my model.
  The Gospel portrays you as praying
  an entire night on the mountain.
  You prayed before working your miracles,
  before choosing your apostles,
  and during the Last Supper.
  You prayed as you sweat blood
  in the garden of Gethsemane;
  you prayed during your agony on the cross.
  You, the Incarnate Word,
  prayed also with the Scripture.
  Your existence was one continuous prayer.
You turned toward your Father with a loving heart,
  and everything was in the service of God's glory:
  "Hallowed be thy name,
  thy kingdom come."
  You ardently awaited the coming of your hour
  in order to accomplish your sacrifice of love.
  You said,

"I and the Father are one."
"Pray without growing weary."
"I always do what pleases my Father."
You help me to understand that unceasing prayer
is communion with the Father,
and in practice, it always consists
in doing the Father's will.

Cf. Lk 6:9–10; Jn 10:30; Lk 22:40; Jn 8:29

*Pray
always*

God and the work for God

Because of your infinite love for me, Lord,
 you called me to follow you,
 to be your child and your disciple.

Then you entrusted me with a unique mission
 that has the same requirements as every mission:
 that I be your apostle and witness.

Still, my experience has taught me
 that I confuse these two realities:
 God and God's work.

God gave me the responsibility
 to carry out certain works—
 some sublime and others more modest;
 some noble and others more common.

And so, with a commitment to pastoral work
 in parishes and with young people in schools,
 with artists and laborers,
 in the world of the press, radio, and television,
 I gave my entire energy to everything
 and poured out all my abilities.
 I did not spare anything,
 not even my life.

But, while I was so passionately
 immersed in action,
 I met the defeat of ingratitude,
 the refusal to collaborate,

the incomprehension of friends,
the lack of support from leaders,
illness and infirmity,
insufficient resources...

And, then when I happened to enjoy success,
when I was the object of everyone's approval,
praise, and affection,
I was suddenly transferred to another position.
So there I was, dazed,
groping about as if in the dark of night:

Why, Lord, are you abandoning me?
I do not want to desert your work
I want to complete it.
I must finish building the Church...
Why do others attack your work?
Why do they withdraw their support?

Kneeling before your altar,
close to the Eucharist,
I heard your answer, Lord:

*"It is me you are supposed to be following,
not my work!
If I will it, you will finish the work entrusted
to you.
It matters little who takes over
your work after you;
that is my business.
Your business is to choose me!"*

*God and the
work for God*

The hidden Jesus

Jesus, you were neither a sorcerer nor magician.
  Every day, in the midst of the crowds,
  with your disciples and apostles,
  you ate and drank and taught...

Some said you were John the Baptist or Elijah.
  Others called you Master, Lord, Son of David.
  Some people considered you a reactionary,
  an agitator of the people,
  a friend of swindlers, publicans,
    and the demon-possessed...

Even those who were closest to you were mistaken.
  Seeing the mobs gathering around you,
  your relatives thought you had gone mad
  and wanted to take you home.
  The disciples on the road to Emmaus
  mistook you for a traveler.
  Magdalene believed you to be the gardener.
  The apostles thought you were a ghost.

You often proclaimed
  that you were sent by the Father.
  Why were there so few people who understood
  and who recognized you?

You were too strange,
  too unimaginably good and generous!
  You pardoned! You loved!

You were so simple!
A messiah should act differently.
The people wanted a God who conformed
to their notions of deity:
majestic and powerful,
calling down fire from heaven,
proclaiming himself king,
leading his disciples in a massacre of the enemy,
and stoning the adulteress.
God had to belong to their party
if God was going to be useful to them.
If the Lord did not know how to behave,
then they had no alternative
but to re-educate him.

The hidden
Jesus

The messenger of the Gospel

An apostle, a missionary, an evangelist need to be prayerful individuals. Perhaps it seems exaggerated to expect such active people to be profoundly prayerful—an aspect of Christian life often considered reserved for contemplative or cloistered religious.

But taking St. Paul as an example, we see that he was a prophet and a missionary that far surpassed everyone as regards activity and work. Yet, Paul was also a mystic. He wrote, *"For me to die is gain";* the close imitation of Christ was the sole concern of his life.

He also wrote: *"For me to live is Christ."* As a missionary of the Gospel, he lived to further the effectiveness of his message. He lived according to the needs of the faithful and to announce the Gospel of Christ.

An authentic missionary must maintain a balance between two tensions: a desire for a mystical interior life, and a desire for missionary activity, which inflames and urges the missionary to go forth to announce salvation in obedience to the Lord's instruction.

"Whether we live or whether we die, we belong to the Lord." An authentic missionary is joyous and calm, because he or she carries a sure hope: *"My earnest expectation and hope is that I shall be ashamed in nothing."*

Cf. Phil 1:21; Rom 14:8; Phil 1:20

The half Christian

At the very least, a Christian is as a person who is baptized, and who may have received a ministry in the Church. There is also, what might be called, the "half Christian."

I am half Christian
  when I am indifferent and without passion
  for the work of the Church.
  I am half Christian
  when my choices are irrational and indecisive,
  when I am a fair weather Christian,
  when I am cowardly and hesitate
    to commit myself
  for fear of complications and failure.
  I am half Christian
  when I am cunning and ready
    to compromise with sin,
  and when I do not dare to tell the truth.

I am an authentic Christian
  when I direct my choices toward the Lord,
  when I fear him and his judgment alone.
  I am an authentic Christian
  when I accept slander, unjust accusations,
    hatred, and rejection,
  but refuse to accept compromising myself
  by conducting my life according
    to godless demands.

I am an authentic Christian
when I maintain a courageous hope,
an ardent faith, and a heroic charity.

If I am not 100 percent Christian, the name
Christian will only attract more misunderstanding
and hatred against Christ and the Church, for I
will be a false messenger.

*The half
Christian*

A challenge for the Church

"But when the Son of Man comes, will he find faith on the earth?"

The Christians of the early Church suffered persecution and death for the faith. History has repeated this down to our own day.

Social sin has become more ferocious, cynical, and destructive than in past centuries. There is more tyranny, more oppression, and more violence. Millions of people weep and plead for justice. This is a challenge flung at the Church. Will we have the strength to come to their aid?

At one time, some people believed that the Marxist revolution was the only way to free humanity. But seventy years of applying that theory has served to discredit it. The challenge still exists however: how to save humanity?

Jesus asked, *"Will there still be faith?"*

With faith people will begin to follow the Lord,
    they will listen to his Word,
    and with it they will overcome the division
    and antagonism between social classes.
    With faith, the power of the strong
    will be at the service of the weak.
    With faith, people will open their hearts
    to the love of God, their Father.
    With faith, all of history and the entire earth
    will be renewed.

Only a love truly built on the foundation of God the Father can conquer hate. Then all people will be brothers and sisters.

In order for this faith to come about, the Church must remain in a state of readiness to announce of the Gospel, in a position to engage in evangelization.

It is only in becoming fully aware of its evangelic mission and missionary responsibility that the Church answers the challenge.

Cf. Lk 18:8

*A challenge
for the Church*

God works in silence

I will let you act, Lord.
  May listening to your Word, who is Christ,
    enrich my life.
  There is nothing you cannot do, Lord.
  You made Abraham and Sarah,
  Zachariah and Elizabeth fruitful.

Silence!
  When you act, we must be silent and listen...
  When you are here, we must be silent,
  abandon our worries,
  and conquer our hesitation.
  The sign that God is at work,
  that God has begun to work,
  is that the people of this world
  are reduced to silence.
  To act in me, Lord,
  you require that I be silent,
  like Mary and Joseph.

I will let you speak, Lord,
  for as long as you wish,
  in the way you wish,
  and at the hour you wish,
  because, Lord Jesus,
  you are the Word itself.
  You will speak when your hour has come.

Perhaps one must wait thirty years...
Indeed, you began to preach
  only after Joseph's death.
But the last word, Lord, will be yours.

*God works
  in silence*

Brief prayers

Lord, you have given me a model for prayer: the *Our Father*. It is brief, concise, and packed with meaning. Your life, Lord, is a sincere and simple prayer addressed to your Father. Your prayer was sometimes long, like your ardent and spontaneous prayer after the Last Supper.

But often your words, those of your mother and apostles were brief, linking together the actions of daily life. I, who often feel weak and indifferent, love to recall those brief prayers before the Eucharist, at my desk, in the street, alone. The more I repeat them, the more they penetrate me. I am close to you, Lord.

Father, forgive them,
  for they know not what they do.
Father, that they may be one.
I am the handmaid of the Lord.
They have no wine.
Behold your son, behold your Mother!
Remember me,
  when you come into your kingdom.
Lord, what do you want me to do?
Lord, you know all things,
  you know that I love you.
Lord, have mercy on me, a poor sinner.

All of these brief prayers, linked one to another, form a life of prayer. Like a chain of discreet gestures, glances, and intimate words, they form a life of love. They keep us in an atmosphere of prayer not distracting us from our present tasks, but helping us to live our day more conscious of God.

Cf. Lk 23:34; Jn 17:22; Lk 1:38; Jn 2:3; Jn 19:26–27; Lk 23:42; Acts 22:10; Jn 21:17; Lk 18:39

Brief prayers

The saints and us

Here are two people who are identical in appearance, living in the same environment, the same situation, and yet, what a difference there can be! Saints might live with me, dwell under the same roof, but they can be as far from me as the heavens are above the earth. Modest, hidden, discreet, few people even take notice of them. But their hearts give forth a light, a fragrance that nothing can overpower.

For an indifferent Christian, holy people seem useless—even difficult to bear or insane!

But saints know the true value of things, and they have chosen the better part. They seem to see so clearly what other people do not see at all or barely perceive. Indeed, they behold everything with the Lord's eyes. The Lord fills their hearts and that is why they are full of love, fidelity, and kindness. They see God and live in the divine presence constantly, trying to always follow the Lord's will.

Because they are filled with God, God works through them.

Instead, filled with my "ego,"
   it seems I only know how to act according
     to my "ego."
The sun shines in its own unique way
   and an oil lamp gives light in a different manner...
   Really, there is nothing so astonishing in this!

The Miracle of Hope

Francis Xavier Nguyen Van Thuan
Political Prisoner, Prophet of Peace
Andre N. Van Chau
Written by a personal friend of Cardinal Van
Thuan, this moving biography chronicles the
life of the man Pope John Paul II says was,
"...marked by a heroic configuration with
Christ on the cross." From a communist jail
cell, to Rome as the leader of the Pontifical
Council for Justice and Peace, Francis Xavier
Nguyen Van Thuan remained a man of
unshakable faith and undying hope.

paperback, approx. 350pp. 16oz/480g
#4822-0 $19.95 ($32.50 Canada)

Testimony of Hope

Cardinal Francis Xavier Nguyen Van Thuan
Here is the complete text of the retreat preached
by Cardinal Van Thuan to John Paul II and the
Roman Curia. Enduring nine years in solitary
confinement—Van Thuan faced what he describes
as "the agonizing pain of isolation and abandonment." In these pages he shares the reality of
hope he discovered through his pain.

paperback, 248pp. 12oz/360g
#7407-8 $15.95 ($25.95 Canada)

The Road of Hope

a gospel from prison
Cardinal Francis Xavier Nguyen Van Thuan
Faced with dire conditions aimed at breaking the
human spirit, Van Thuan secretly wrote hope-filled
notes to the people of his diocese. This holy man's
simplicity and wisdom have inspired thousands to
embrace life with a new faith.

paperback, 248pp. 12oz/360g
#6473-0 $15.95 ($25.95 Canada)

www.pauline.org
800-876-4463 U.S.A.
800-668-2078 Canada

Pauline
BOOKS & MEDIA

Pauline
BOOKS & MEDIA

The Daughters of St. Paul operate book and media centers at the following addresses. Visit, call or write the one nearest you today, or find us on the World Wide Web, www.pauline.org

California
3908 Sepulveda Blvd, Culver City,
  CA 90230   310-397-8676
5945 Balboa Avenue, San Diego,
  CA 92111   858-565-9181
46 Geary Street, San Francisco,
  CA 94108   415-781-5180

Florida
145 S.W. 107th Avenue, Miami,
  FL 33174   305-559-6715

Hawaii
1143 Bishop Street, Honolulu,
  HI 96813   808-521-2731
Neighbor Islands call:
  800-259-8463

Illinois
172 North Michigan Avenue,
  Chicago, IL 60601
  312-346-4228

Louisiana
4403 Veterans Memorial Blvd,
  Metairie, LA 70006
  504-887-7631

Massachusetts
885 Providence Hwy, Dedham,
  MA 02026   781-326-5385

Missouri
9804 Watson Road, St. Louis,
  MO 63126   314-965-3512

New Jersey
561 U.S. Route 1, Wick Plaza,
  Edison, NJ 08817   732-572-1200

New York
150 East 52nd Street, New York,
  NY 10022   212-754-1110
78 Fort Place, Staten Island, NY
  10301   718-447-5071

Pennsylvania
9171-A Roosevelt Blvd, Philadelphia,
  PA 19114   215-676-9494

South Carolina
243 King Street, Charleston, SC
  29401   843-577-0175

Tennessee
4811 Poplar Avenue, Memphis,
  TN 38117   901-761-2987

Texas
114 Main Plaza, San Antonio, TX
  78205   210-224-8101

Virginia
1025 King Street, Alexandria, VA
  22314   703-549-3806

Canada
3022 Dufferin Street, Toronto,
  Ontario, Canada M6B 3T5   416-
  781-9131
1155 Yonge Street, Toronto, Ontario,
  Canada M4T 1W2   416-934-3440

¡También somos su fuente para libros, videos y música en español!